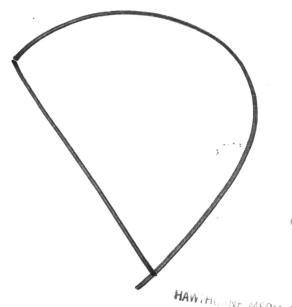

PICTURE LIBRARY

ROBOTS

ROBOTS

N.S. Barrett

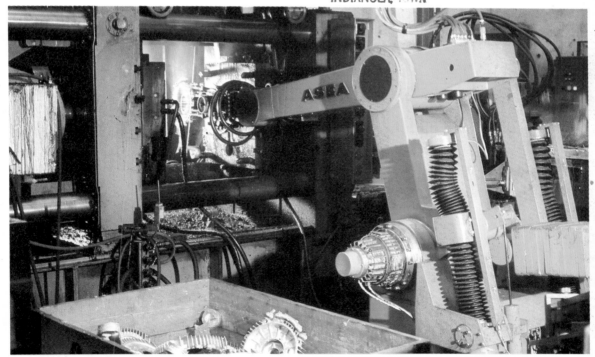

Franklin Watts

London   New York   Sydney   Toronto

© 1985 Franklin Watts Ltd

First published in Great Britain
    1985 by
Franklin Watts Ltd
12a Golden Square
London W1

First published in the USA by
Franklin Watts Inc
387 Park Avenue South
New York
N.Y. 10016

First published in Australia by
Franklin Watts
1 Campbell Street
Artarmon, NSW 2064

UK ISBN: 0 86313 222 7
US ISBN: 0-531-04947-7
Library of Congress Catalog Card
Number: 84 52001

Printed in Italy

Designed by
Barrett & Willard

Photographs by
ASEA
N. S. Barrett
Boeing Commercial Airplane Co
British Telecom
Clayton Bailey, Wonders of
  the World Museum
COI, London
Colne Robotics
Economatics/BBC
Ford Motors
Jessop Microelectronics
L. J. Electronics
McAndroid Ltd
Maplin Electronic Supplies
NASA
Prism Microproducts
Sas Group
Science Museum, London
UK Atomic Energy Authority
University of Southern California
Valiant Designs

Illustrated by
Mike Saunders
Stuart Willard

Technical Consultant
John Lambert

Contents

Introduction

Robots are machines that can do particular jobs. They are usually controlled by computers. In films and comics, robots often look like human machines. But real robots do not look anything like people.

Robots have no brains of their own. They are made to move and work by instructions fed into their computers.

△ Flying sparks do not bother this factory robot. Robots are used to do many jobs that people might find unpleasant.

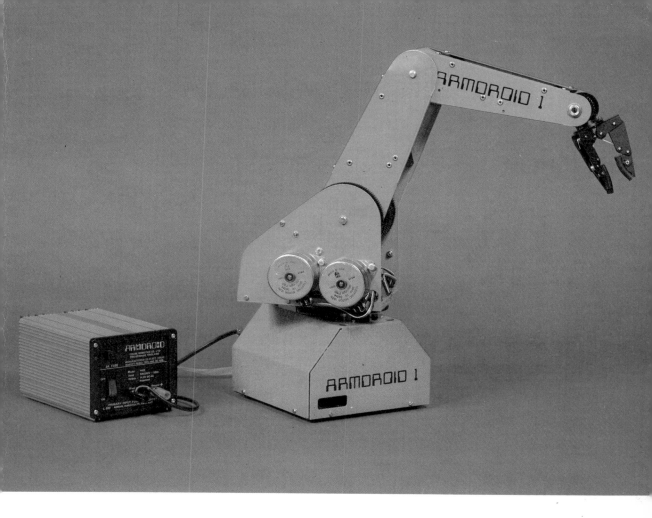

The simplest robot may be just a mechanical arm. But some robots have legs, wheels or tracks. Robots with a television camera can "see". Some robots can also be made to "hear", "feel" and "speak".

Most robots perform useful tasks, such as making cars or flying planes. But you can also build robots as a hobby.

△ Small robots may be made up from special kits. They are used at home or in school, or even in factories.

The robot

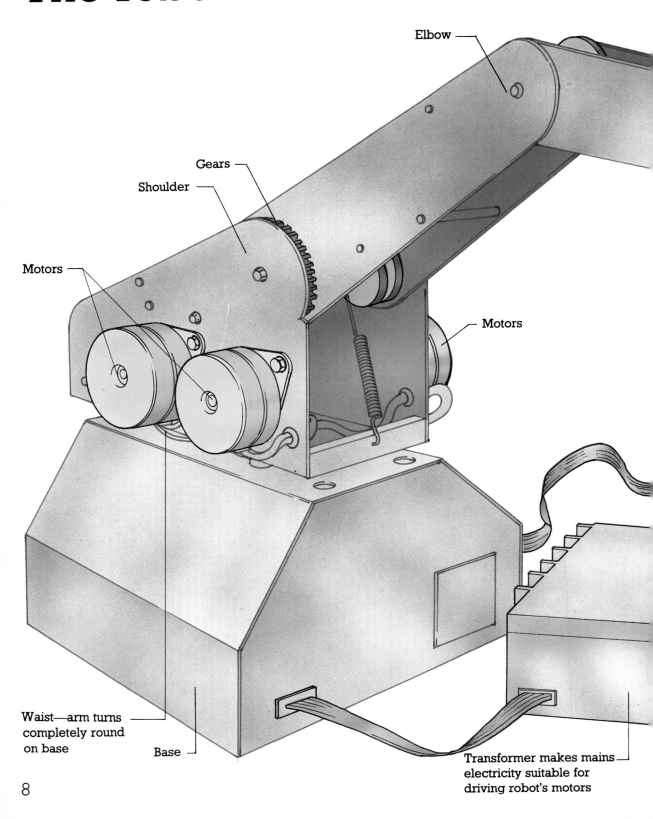

Elbow

Gears

Shoulder

Motors

Motors

Waist—arm turns completely round on base

Base

Transformer makes mains electricity suitable for driving robot's motors

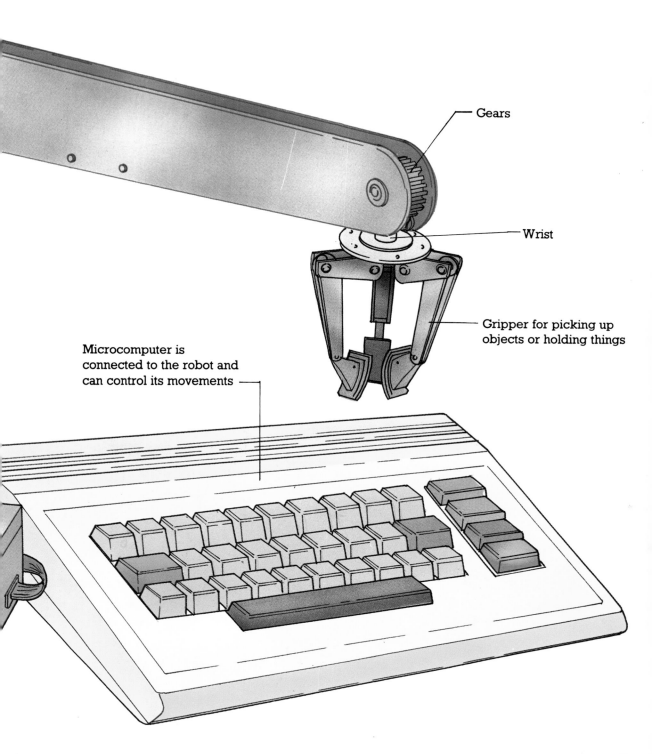

Gears

Wrist

Gripper for picking up
objects or holding things

Microcomputer is
connected to the robot and
can control its movements

How a robot works

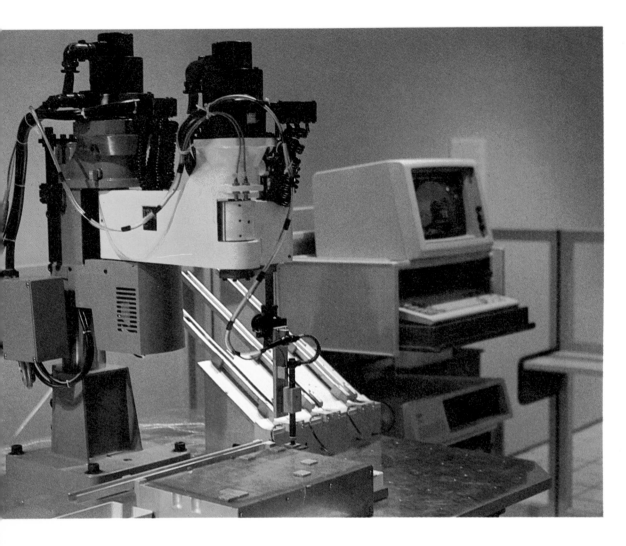

Robots used in factories are called industrial robots. Simple robots are used to pick up objects and place them in position. These are called pick-and-place robots. They do jobs that people find boring. They can carry on working without any rest.

△ A pick-and-place robot sets metal squares into position. The computer that controls the operations is on the right.

Robots need motors to make them work. First, directions are fed into a computer. This is called programming. The computer is connected to the robot and controls its motors. Different motors control the various movements of the robot.

A robot arm may have a gripper, a magnet or a suction pad to pick objects up. A tool such as a drill can also be fitted to the robot arm.

▽ The joints of a robot allow it to move in several different ways. These are called "degrees of freedom." A robot with six degrees of freedom is shown in the diagrams.

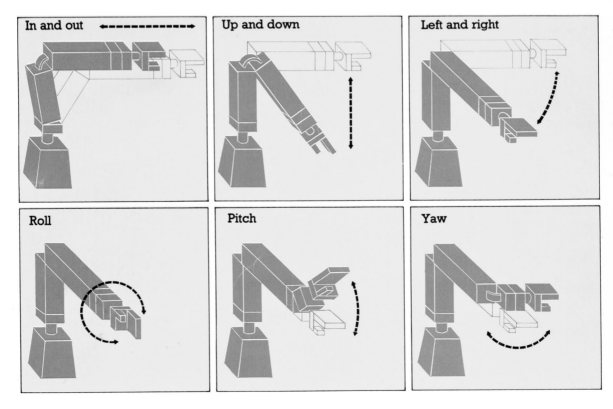

In and out

Up and down

Left and right

Roll

Pitch

Yaw

Robots that make

Most robots are built for work in factories. About half of these are used for welding. This is a method of joining metal parts by using great heat. It is very important in making automobiles. Robots can weld faster than human workers. Their work is also more reliable than even expert welders.

▷ A robot handling parts in an automobile factory. It is using a suction gripper to pick up metal discs.

▽ A small industrial robot smooths out bumps and ridges on plastic parts.

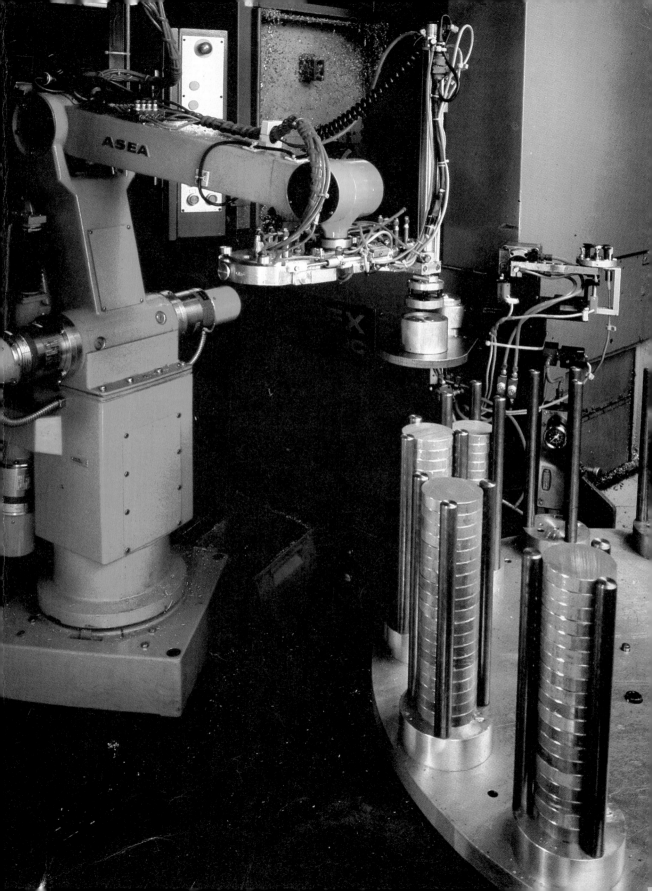

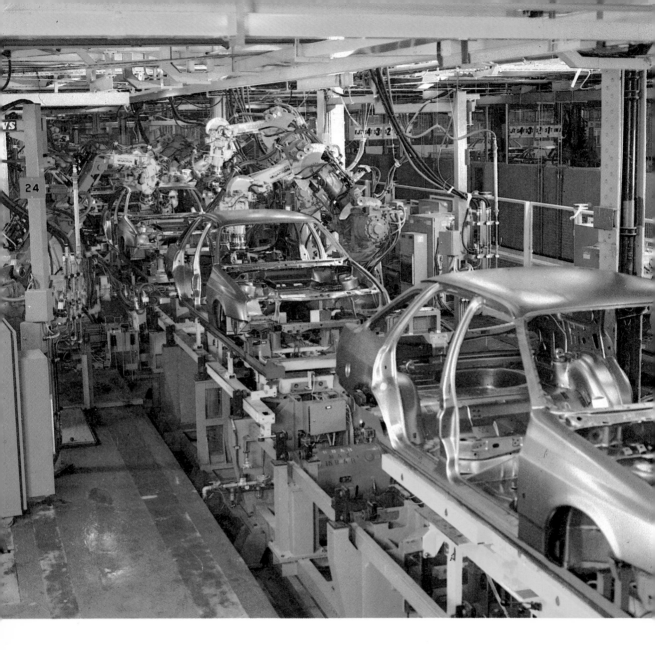

Another important factory job done by robots is paint spraying. They are also used to load hot plastics or metal into machines that press them into shapes. None of these are pleasant jobs for people to do.

△ There is not a human being to be seen as these car bodies pass through lines of robots.

Robots that guide

Special kinds of robots take the place of human beings in guiding ships and planes. They are called automatic pilots.

These are not like other robots because they are programmed to do just one special job. They are really computers. All the information they need is fed into them and they control the speed and direction of the ship or plane.

▽ You cannot see an automatic pilot. It is like an invisible robot. The pilot just flips a switch on the flight deck, and the plane flies itself. An automatic pilot flies a plane more accurately than a human pilot.

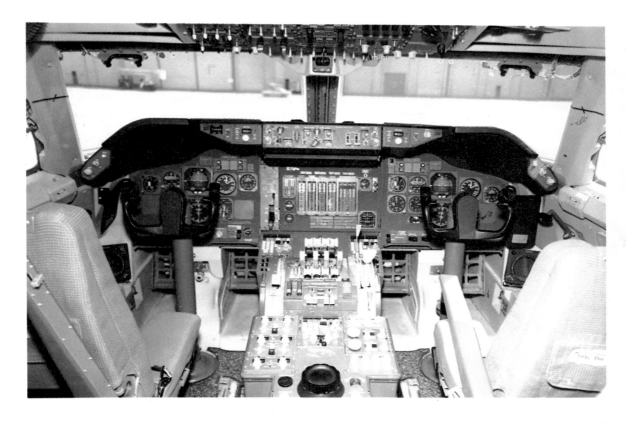

Robots in space

Working in space is very difficult and dangerous for human beings. They have to wear bulky space suits and carry their own supply of air to breathe. In the future, robots will probably be used to work on space stations and on the planets. The unmanned spacecraft that have been sent into space are also kinds of robots. Some of the craft that have been used to find out about the moon and planets are robots too.

▷ A Viking lander on the planet Mars. Robots like this are landed on the planets to send information back to Earth. They have television cameras to send back pictures, and all kinds of other instruments for studying the planet.

▽ An arm of the Viking lander scoops up soil from the surface of Mars. The lander had equipment to test the soil, but no signs of life were found.

Danger!

Many people have to do very dangerous jobs. Robots are beginning to take over some of these jobs. They can stand great heat or explosions. They can work safely with dangerous chemicals. And they can work in places that are too dangerous for human beings.

△ A special robot, called a Wheelbarrow, is used by soldiers in the British Army for dangerous tasks such as checking for bombs or mines.

Most of the robots used for dangerous work are controlled from a distance. This is called remote control. The operator sends the robot to the point of danger.

Remote-controlled robots can be equipped with a television camera, which sends pictures back to the operator. A soldier operating such a robot might be able to use it to make an unexploded bomb or mine safe.

▽ Another dangerous task robots can do is fight fires. This Hunter robot is also used for bomb disposal work.

Robots are used for underwater work. They can check and repair cables and pipelines at the bottom of the sea. They do heavy work such as drilling and welding. They may also help to look after oil rigs.

Some people work with materials that give off deadly radiations. Special robots are now being used to handle these materials.

▽ A Seadog robot is lowered into the water. It has special tracks for moving along the sea bed. It is used to bury cables and to check and repair them.

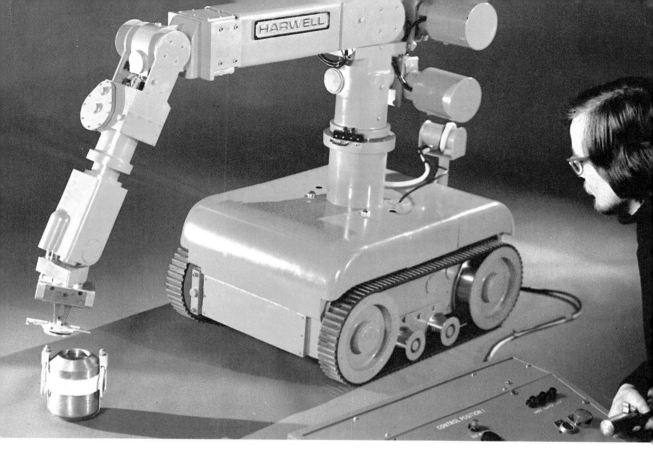

△A scientist demonstrates how a remote-controlled robot can handle dangerous chemicals. The robot, called Roman, runs on tracks.

◁A scientist operates remote-controlled arms. There is a safe thickness of lead glass between him and the deadly radiation inside the chamber.

Robots that teach

Designing and building robots has become a popular hobby. Many people now have home computers. You can buy special kits to build your own personal robot and link it up to your computer.

Floor-crawling robots called turtles are used in schools to help teach subjects such as geometry. Special robots are built to teach people about robotics, the science of robots.

▷Hero 1 is a robot used for teaching robotics.

▽Turtle robots are used for many things, from drawing simple shapes to playing tunes. They follow directions given in computer language.

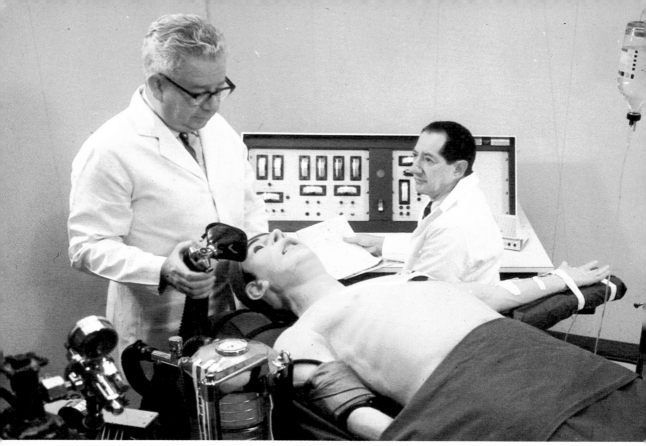

△Special robots have been designed for doctors to practice on. They are lifelike dummies that can be programmed to behave like human beings when examined and operated on.

◁The BBC Buggy is one of the best robots for learning how to use a computer to control robots, and for learning to understand robotics.

Fun robots

Robots have always been popular toys. At first, they were just dolls that worked mechanically. But today robot toys are more like real robots. They help you to understand how real robots work. Many robots are designed for exhibitions or for use in films and videos.

△ Robo 1 has hand controls, but its arm moves like a real robot's.

◁ These toy robots are just mechanical men.

▷ Two robots made for an exhibition. The larger one on the right is called On-Off.

▽ These mini-robots are made up from kits. They work by remote control. They can climb, crawl or spin round.

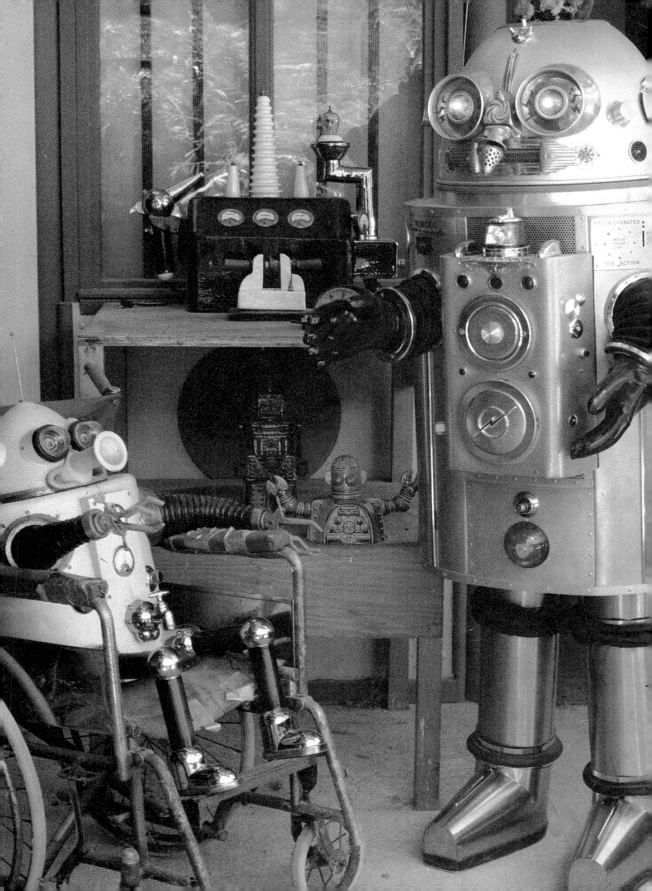

The story of robots

Robots in stories

The idea of robots has excited people for a long time. Everyone likes the thought of having mechanical creatures to do all the boring and difficult work. But in stories, robots often threaten to take over their owners. In some stories, though, the robots are friendly, helpful characters.

The first robots

The first robots looked nothing like the robots of stories and films. In fact, the first automatic machines were not thought of as robots. The word had not even been invented. Two hundred years ago, Oliver Evans built a mill in the United States that used automatic machinery. This was the start of automation.

In France in 1801, Joseph Jacquard invented a loom that used cards punched with holes to make patterned silk. These cards were the first computer "programs." The holes in the cards were the instructions that the machine needed to weave patterns.

△ An early automated factory.

△ On a Jacquard loom, the punched cards controlled the patterns.

Androids

The word robot was first used in a play written over sixty years ago. The play, by a Czech writer called Karel Capek, was titled *R.U.R.* This stands for Rossum's Universal Robots. The word robot came from a Czech word meaning drudge or slave. The story was about a scientist, Dr Rossum, who produced artificial people in a factory. But, like Frankenstein's monster in another story, the robots turned

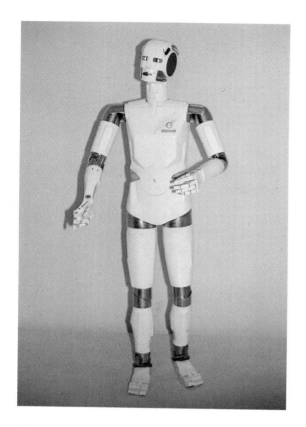

△ McAndroid—a modern android.

against their maker. Robots like these, which are made in human form, are called androids.

Putting robots to work

The first robot that could be programmed to do different tasks was built in 1954 by an American inventor called George Devol. He got together with Joseph Engelberger, who founded the Unimation company. They made the world's first robots to work in industry.

The robot brain

The robot's brain is a computer. The computer used with the first robots allowed them to do only simple jobs. But as computers were improved, robots could be. programmed to do more skilled work, such as welding.

△ Using a turtle to draw shapes.

Turtles

Many people today have small computers in their homes. Robots are now made that can be linked to these home computers. One type of robot is the turtle. Turtles are used in schools to help pupils understand simple geometry and computer language.

Facts and records

Japan leads

Japan and the United States make most of the world's industrial robots. But out of the world's total "population" of about 40,000 robots, Japan has over 16,000, twice the number at work in the United States. The Japanese aim in the future to have robots doing all the work in their big factories.

Robots that see

Robots equipped with cameras can "see." The problem is to

△ A robot that can "see" checks a car part for faults.

teach a robot to understand what it sees. For example, a robot's computer cannot recognize a picture of a flower as well as the human brain can. But robots can be taught to recognize simple shapes. This is useful, for example, in checking flaws in automobile parts.

Teaching robots

Robot engineers "teach" robots how to do their work. They use special teach units. These move each joint of the robot in the right direction. The engineer presses a button on the unit to record each movement in the robot's memory. In this way a robot can be taught to make a complicated series of movements.

Asimov's laws

The American author Isaac Asimov features robots in many of his science fiction stories. He made three rules for his robots: (1) A robot may not injure a human being or allow one to come to harm. (2) A robot must obey orders given it by human beings except when such orders would break the first rule. (3) A robot must protect itself as long as this does not make it break one of the other rules.

Glossary

Android
A robot that looks like a human being and in many ways behaves like one.

Automation
The method of running a factory or other business by machines that need little or no attention from human workers.

Gripper
A part that can be connected to a robot's wrist. It is used to pick up or hold objects. Grippers have two or more "fingers."

Industrial robot
A robot used in a factory.

Pick-and-place robot
A robot used for jobs such as sorting, packing or assembling parts. It picks up objects and puts them in the correct place.

Pitch
The movement of a robot's wrist in an up-and-down direction.

Programming
Feeding instructions into a computer. A robot's computer is programmed so that the robot will perform a particular task or series of operations.

Remote control
Controlling a robot or machine from a distance. Robots used for underwater work or checking for bombs, for example, are remote-controlled. These are not free-moving robots. They depend on human instructions.

Robot arm
A robot that works like a human arm. Most industrial robots and many others are robot arms.

Robotics
The science and study of robots and how to use and improve them.

Roll
The movement of a robot's wrist in a circular, sideways motion.

Turtle
A robot that moves on wheels and responds to directions given in computer language.

Welding
Joining metal parts together by heating them to a high temperature.

Yaw
The movement of a robot's wrist in a left or right direction.

Index